Echoes *of old* *China*

Traditional beliefs and values • Trea Wiltshire

FormAsia

Echoes of old China

Published by FormAsia Books Limited
706 Yu Yuet Lai Building
45 Wyndham Street
Central, Hong Kong

Published 2001
Written by Trea Wiltshire
Edited by Zenobia Barlow
Proofread by James Cox
Photographed by Benno Gross and
    Kwan Kwong Chung
Designed by Lilian Tang Design Limited
Label Designs, courtesy of Joel Chung
© Text copyright, FormAsia Books Limited
Printed by Sing Cheong Printing Co. Limited
Printed in Hong Kong

ISBN No. 962-7283-47-9

CONTENTS

links with an almost fabled past

The emperors of imperial China frequently discouraged, and occasionally banned, migration from the Middle Kingdom, frowning on unworthy subjects who abandoned the tombs of their ancestors. However, the promise of trade – or the need to flee the ravages of warlords or civil war, famine or flood – began luring the sons and daughters of China across oceans as soon as there were junks sturdy enough to carry them.

Well before the adventurous Admiral Cheng Ho led imperial naval expeditions to Southeast Asia in the 15th century, expanding China's sphere of influence and gathering tributes to the Son of Heaven, Chinese traders were familiar with ports from Malacca to Manila. And when European powers began to chase the riches of the East – silks and spices, and later tea and opium – a string of prosperous colonial ports offered new opportunities that widened the web of Chinese trade.

By the 19th century, European nations had established far-flung possessions from the Indian Ocean to the South China Sea, and the

sea lanes that linked these ports with the wider
world were a further conduit for migration.

Stamford Raffles turned the fishing village of
Singapore into a thriving port, but it was the
Chinese who effected the transformation, soon
equalling and later outnumbering the native
Malays. And, when the Union Jack rose above a
forgotten corner of the Manchu empire, giving
birth to the British Crown Colony of Hong Kong,
the entrepot port was quickly dominated by
Chinese compradors and traders from the mainland.

Traders at heart, opportunistic by nature, Chinese migrants were soon boarding steamships to venture further afield, to the rough and ready goldtowns of Canada, America and Australia. Some travelled on their own account, others were herded into unsanitary, overcrowded vessels that carried a human cargo of indentured labourers to wherever there was a demand for their labour.

Most migrants hailed from China's southern maritime provinces, Kwangtung and Fukien, where mountainous terrain and unpromising soils had forced migrants to leave their ancestral villages for centuries. Whenever the tea gardens or rice paddies failed to produce a crop sufficient to sustain the clans that lived within walled villages, locals would estimate the number of men who would need to sell their labour in a foreign land. A successful harvest was a double cause for celebration, for there would be no need for the clan to say farewell to one of its sons.

As soon as an indentured labourer had won his freedom to work on his own account, or a migrant began to earn – prospecting leases rejected by white miners, labouring tirelessly on transcontinental railways, or working as laundryman, cook, or market gardener – he would send money back to his village.

These pioneer settlers never forgot the emperor's admonition about abandoning the graves of their ancestors, nor did they sever links with clan villages where every member shared a common surname. Their patient toil and frugal mode of living invariably meant that they soon consolidated their fragile footholds in the foreign land. They were the first in a chain of migration with links to the ancestral village, where others tended the family graves and burnt incense before the tablets of ancestors.

When a settler's survival was ensured, he would send for a son to help run a fledgling business, and other relatives would soon swell the outpost that the Tangs or Wongs had established far from home. Most dreamed of returning to China but countless died far from home, comforted by the knowledge that their

bones would be returned to a final resting place in China.

As the migrants put down new roots, Chinatowns mushroomed in cities across the world. Temples with upturned eaves and porcelain tiled roofs displayed a familiar pantheon of gods; open-air markets duplicated the colour and clamour of those back home; and at festival times, homes were decorated with the bright paper lanterns that were already being fashioned by a craftsman that hailed from a clan village.

Today the Chinese diaspora numbers well over 30 million people. Many live in well-appointed suburbs in the great cities of the world; others cling to the Chinatowns with their familiar sights, sounds and smells. But even the well-suited young computer executive from the smart end of town finds time to duck into an herbalist's shop for a cocktail of snake bile, while his wife, in designer jeans, will be drawn by the silks and jades on offer in small distinctive shops. For these are links with a homeland their great grandfather left, and which they may never have visited.

In the context of cities such as Beijing or San Francisco, Hong Kong or Singapore – where expansive shop windows are filled with every imaginable indulgence – these small Chinese shops are essentially modest. They sell merchandise that the Chinese have always valued, in much the same way as in earlier generations. Their trading names and merchandise are carved on wooden boards in bold calligraphy, faded perhaps to mellow gold on red.

As you enter you are drawn back into another era by huge gilt-framed mirrors discoloured with age, and sepia portraits of a grandfather who left China to seek prosperity in a foreign city. There may be polished wood, touches of brass, an occasional blackwood chair, framed testimonials from satisfied customers (each one a story worth hearing) or an appropriate couplet of high moral tone expressed in the finest calligraphy.

In these shops there is often time to exchange niceties over a cup of fragrant tea, to savour the lingering sense of formality and unhurried gentility that is a world away from the brash salesmanship of the surrounding cities.

The stories of the shops themselves soon become familiar. Most originated with a great grandfather who fled the turmoil of China's famines, war-lords or civil wars. He came with little, but put to work the skills acquired from his own father, starting perhaps with a small stall in a narrow street. By the time his son took over the business, they had generally moved to a better location, a proper shop. The founder of the

business, whose portrait hangs on the wall, was buried in China, as was his son. But the current owner's father won't go back to China to die. With roots in a land that once felt foreign, he now feels at home. Business is good but there is no need for a bigger shop, he says. Who would run it? His children are studying computer sciences and engineering at the university.

a taste for
tea

Legend suggests that the
very first brew of China tea
was accidental. A fortuitous
breeze plucked the leaves of
wild tea trees and deposited
them in a bowl of boiling
water being prepared for an
emperor, 5,000 years ago.
Tempted by the aroma, the
emperor sampled the infusion
and was well pleased with its
soothing, reviving qualities.
A tradition – and an industry
– were thus born.

By the seventh century the custom of drying and smoking the leaves of the evergreen *Camellia sensesis* was well established. Tea gardens flourished in many provinces and already the emperor received an annual tribute of tea from his subjects – a custom that survived to the last imperial dynasty.

However ten centuries elapsed before the brew the Chinese called "t'e" or "ch'a" became fashionable in Europe.

Initially sold in Britain as a luxury cure-all, China tea soon became indispensable to the English way of life. Taken in the late afternoon it was said to dispel what the Duke of Bedford's wife described as "that sinking feeling."

Tea connoisseurs were soon rhapsodizing over the subtle variations of teas grown in different regions, for both soil and climate imparted different flavours. With countless varieties available, tea tasters sometimes blended up to 40 different teas to create the taste to tempt a fickle market. And when the market insisted on "new season" teas, the mighty clipper ships raced before the northeast monsoons in a bid to win the best prices in 19th century London.

It was soon clear that the benison of tea was a mixed blessing, for it threatened to deplete Britain's coffers of silver – until the taipans of the tea trade began smuggling opium into China. The potent sap of the poppy from British India balanced the China trade, and ensured that both tea and opium dominated the early years of the newly-acquired British Crown Colony of Hong Kong.

Since the 7th century, the Chinese have dried and smoked the leaf from mountain tea gardens, savouring the infusion it created.

Whereas tea-drinking in London's Belgrave Square was accompanied by polite conversation over trays laden with silver at precisely the same hour every day, in China the view was that almost any time was teatime.

Teahouses ranged from the simple to the luxurious, the latter luring customers with singsong girls, story-telling, music, miniature gardens and fine

Like scholars and painters of the Ming dynasty, Hong Kong entrepreneur Dr. K. S. Lo collected the red and purple stoneware that takes its name from Yixing, a town in China that has a long tradition in creating beauty. Today in Hong Kong, the time-honoured ritual of taking tea begins with a visit to a traditional teashop, its pewter canisters and loft packed with a variety of fragrant brews from China.

porcelain. While such refinement added to the ambience of a fashionable teahouse, a noisy congestion characterised more basic establishments.

Taking *yum cha* at a teahouse generally meant doing a bit of business, gossiping and enjoying the *dim sum* – savoury delicacies such as transparent pouches of dough filled with minced shrimp – that appeared on every table. The *dim sum* nestled in

small round bamboo baskets that are stacked for steaming. The Chinese character for *dim sum* literally meant "touching the heart" and this they clearly did, for the bamboo baskets were emptied and replaced at a rapid rate!

Some teahouses catered specifically to bird-lovers who gathered to show off a new cage or the songbird within it. Birdwalking was an ancient custom and the teahouse became an obvious destination – particularly if it attracted bird-fanciers who could debate the merits of skylarks from Mongolia or flycatchers from Thailand.

Dim sum, the savoury delicacies served in teahouses, nestle in small round bamboo baskets that are stacked one on top of the other for steaming. Synthetic containers cannot compete – for the bamboo imparts a flavour of its own to the *dim sum*, enabling a centuries-old craft to survive.

Meanwhile the birds vied vocally from a variety of beautifully-crafted cages suspended above their owners. Their trilling and caroling added a sweet cadence to the shrilling of waitresses and the clattering of dishes.

Sometimes in the teahouse there was *mahjong* – the slap of ivory or bamboo tiles added yet another dimension of noise – but always there was talk and tea. Unlike tea-drinkers in Europe who favoured black fermented teas, the Chinese preferred fragrant green tea, or the partly-fermented oolong teas. Gunpowder was a particular favourite, its smoky flavour heightened by the fresh tang of mint leaves; pale gold Jasmine was another, sweetened by the scent of flower petals. And the names of the different varieties – Cloud Mist, Dragon Well, *Po Lei*, *Lapsang Souchong* – were an added source of pleasure.

And when the pot was finished, but the conversation was not, the lid was simply set askew and a replacement appeared, made, whenever possible, from the "heavenly water" gathered in huge jars set beneath the teahouse eaves.

In China taking tea in a teahouse had, since ancient times, added pleasure to the pattern of daily life.

the Chinese dragon

The Dragon had always been China's most potent symbol.

He lived in the East, source of the winds that carried fertile dust to enrich the fields. His season was spring, when his warm breath quickened new growth in the sere winter earth. His voice was terrible, reverberating in thunder, but it carried with it the blessing of rain. He dwelt in cavernous mountains or the fathomless depths of the ocean, but rose to ride the billowing rainclouds, his talons lancing the earth with the lightning of summer storms. His serpentine neck, bulging eyes and

writing opalescent scales created an awesome spectacle – and the people were ever mindful of his presence, in the air or beneath the earth. So they built their white-washed houses low, so as not to impede his flight, and on sites that would not adversely affect the *"Ch'i"* or spiritual breath of the universe. For the Dragon – its force positive and creative and male – embodied the element of Yang, one of two basic components of the Chinese cosmos.

The Dragon was also the spirit of the ancient land.

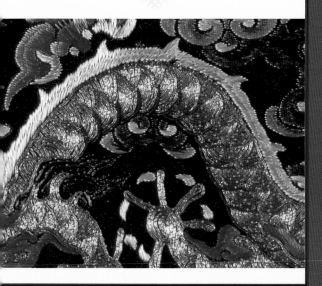

a *philosophy of.*
cosmic
balance

In China the ebb and flow of a
man's fortune simply reflected
the eternal shift of unseen
forces – conflicting in times
of crises, then coalescing into
harmony. The elements that
were the pulse of the cosmos
– Yang and Yin, sun and
moon, light and dark, heaven
and earth, male and female –
sought a union that expressed
their essential differences
while accommodating them
within the embrace of a
single entity: The Taoist
symbol circle.

I n the long memory of the land and its people there were countless tales of the consequences of disharmony: of monsoon-swollen rivers swallowing entire villages; of endless droughts when river beds dried and people went hungry. But there was always the patient conviction that harmony would be restored. Such harmony, in nature and in man, was born of a balance of Yin and Yang.

The Chinese believed there was much a man could do to enhance the balance of forces and to shape a fortune that was moulded, on a daily basis, by a myriad of unseen powers.

Ancestors, temple gods, earth gods – plus the animistic spirits that inhabited an ancient banyan tree or an outcrop of rock pasted over with crimson-papered prayers – all had the power to influence a man's destiny.

The temple god, gaudy and terrible on an altar laden with offerings, might listen to the heart that was unburdened beneath his gaze. His appearance might be formidable, but he had an acknowledged weakness for sweet incense and the incessant attention of those who sought his help.

Temple gods presiding over altars laden with offerings have an acknowledged weakness for sweet incense and the incessant attention of those who seek their help.

34

Departed spirits are offered holidays from hell and paper replicas of home comforts – from elaborate gowns to luxury cars – that can be purchased from paper shops.

He might ease the poverty of a coolie whose rice bowl was seldom full and whose body was wasted by the solace of opium – a coolie who would surely have died unnoticed but for the pity of the gods.

Elaborately handcrafted paper creations turn paper shops and temple forecourts into colourful reminders that life is merely an audition for death. Flames will eventually destroy these fanciful paper luxuries, carrying them to waiting spirits.

Or he might increase the wealth of a shopkeeper who had never failed to please him and whose fortune he had guided from a humble streetstall (where a tiny shrine was never without incense) to an open-fronted shop on a busy street where the altar and its ever present offerings were bathed in the red glow of prosperity.

Within the temples, Buddhist deities often shared a shrine with a Taoist counterpart, for these two religions – plus Confucianism – provided the core of an eclectic mix.

Confucian philosophy formed the solid ethical base of a well-ordered society that respected both elders and ancestors. Buddhism, imported from India, added notions of reincarnation and purgatory, modified by the innate impulse to better one's lot – in life and death. So departed spirits were offered holidays from hell and in the temple forecourt paper replicas of home comforts – from cars to consorts – were burnt to make life in the underworld more tolerable. Finally Taoist magic – from exorcism to the manipulation of malevolent spirits – added its own dimension to a blend of beliefs which perfectly reflected the expectations of its creators.

When China was devastated by floods or famine, the people knew that the fine balance of Yin Yang forces had been disturbed. And when the miniature cosmos of the body suffered a similar imbalance – "too much fire," the physician would say, or "too much water" – a man inevitably succumbed to ailments ranging from the rheumatic aches of "wind in the bones" or a disappointing decline in masculine vigour.

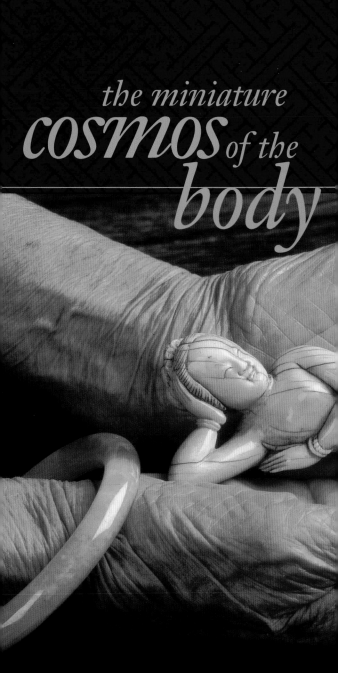

the miniature
COSMOS of the
body

Traditional Chinese medicine was governed by the philosophy of cosmic balance already widely embraced. The body was divided into Yin and Yang organs, each affiliated to one of the Five Elements (wood, earth, fire, metal and water) that also played a vital role in shaping a man's fortune.

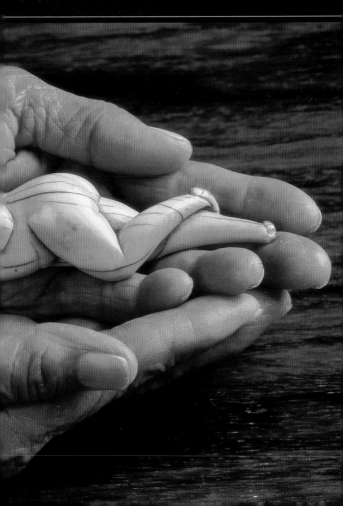

T he heart was a Yin organ generating energy and was thus affiliated with fire; the stomach, a Yang organ, nurtured the body and was therefore related to earth.

The physician based his diagnosis on interpreting the pulse rate and observing the facial features of his patient. His aim was to restore the body's balance by prescribing a blend of ingredients that might include herbs, bark, roots, powders, seeds, fossils, bones, minerals, animal organs, lichens, seaweed, seahorses, insects, antlers and even bat's dung.

The ingredients were wrapped in leaves, or folded

With over 2,000 different herbs and substances – bark and roots, fossils and sea horses, insects and antlers – secreted in the drawers of Chinese medicine shops, the traditional pharmacopoeia continues to offer infinite hope to those in need.

The bonesetter's rooms in Shanghai Street afford a glimpse into a fast-disappearing world of healing, eclipsed by the X-ray and modern medicine. Beyond its shuttered doors, carved blackwood chairs line the wall beneath the fading testimonials of customers.

Special blends of herbs, and precious pain-killing balms – distilled from the musk of deer and the gall bladders of bear – fill the brass canisters that gleam in the cool interior of the bonesetter's establishment. Faded ancient tracts are still relevant in a declining profession where skills are handed down from master to apprentice, father to son.

in packages, with instructions regarding their preparation. Others were prepared in the traditional medicine shop, where the patient consumed his therapeutic brew on the spot.

In some cases the prescribed medicine came from a nearby snake shop, for both the blood and bile of snakes were considered beneficial. Cobras, vipers and other deadly reptiles writhed in close-packed wooden drawers until an experienced handler removed one and relieved it of its bile – which was conveniently replaced for further prescriptions.

While the curative properties of many Chinese medicines were widely recognized, some seemed to be selected more for their sexual symbolism. Confronted, as was common, by a wife and a string of expectant concubines, those experiencing a disappointing decline in libido sought refuge in the extraordinary selection of materia medica displayed in the traditional medicine shops. The antlers of deer, reputed to be the only animal to have located a sacred fungus bestowing immortality, were cut, dried and sliced or boiled to distil the essence. And if the antlers failed there were alternative remedies from the stag's phallus to dried caterpillars, or the fiery tonic prepared from wild ginseng. While the wealthy could afford the wild ginseng root from the forests of Manchuria and Korea, the man in the street contented himself with the cultivated variety.

With over 10,000 different herbs and substances in the traditional pharmacopoeia, medicine shops – like Chinese temples – offered infinite hope for those in need.

a man's *fortune*

Once health was restored, the patient would give thanks both to the physician and the deities at the local temple that had a hand in restoring the balance of the body. In fact the business of acknowledging the influence of the gods was so much a part of daily life that the temple itself held none of the awesome formality of a church.

A woman might call at the temple to burn joss sticks at the shrine of a favourite god while on her way to market, having first tended the shrines of earth gods on the outskirts of her village. In the temple square old men read papers, gossiped or played dice in the sunshine. On temple steps worn smooth by the passage of naked feet, women and cripples begged – for those who came to request favours of the gods would wish to appear virtuous.

A porcelain dragon pursuing the pearl of wisdom that all men seek might ornament the ridge of the temple's tiled rooftop, and in the cool of its interior, the slow coil of incense scented the air. Brass urns gleamed, walls were blackened by the smoke of countless offerings, a gong sounded and the candles' glow lit the sheen of a deity's embroidered gown.

In the dim tranquillity, the village or town receded and the dominant sound became the gentle rhythmic shaking of the *chim* by the kneeling worshippers. As single bamboo slivers slipped to the floor, messages from the gods were revealed.

A great deal of fortune-telling went on in the temple for the fortune-teller could interpret the

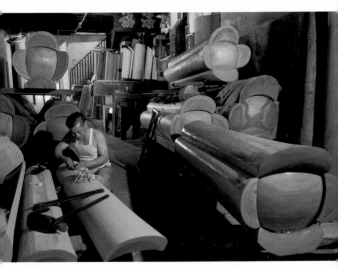

unseen forces that were constantly at work. He did this in a variety of ways: by interpreting the *chim* sticks in relations to the prayer offered; by consulting the Almanac that dictated the tasks that should or should not be undertaken in any one day; and by reading palms and facial features. Moles and blemishes were all significant in physiognomy and much faith was placed in this form of fortune-telling.

In China, a man of wealth would once have acquired a coffin decades before his death – choosing the finest camphor, regularly lacquered to achieve an awesome sheen. Coffin-makers now work mainly with imported Chinese pine, dyed yellow and waxed to an enchancing golden hue.

In high-rise high-tech cities messages are still conveyed to the gods on the smoke of sweet-smelling incense. Turning ground sandalwood into joss sticks is one of China's oldest industries, and one that may well have given the island its name, Fragrant Harbour.

Fortune-tellers were consulted before any important decisions were taken, particularly if they related to birth, marriage or death.

When a man died his spirit took a triple form: one accompanied the body to the grave in a coffin

A great deal of fortune-telling went on in the temple for the fortune-teller could interpret the unseen forces that were constantly at work. He did this in a variety of ways: by interpreting the *chim* sticks; by consulting the Almanac that dictated the tasks that should or should not be undertaken in any one day; and by reading palms and facial features

carved from Chinese pine; another traveled to the underworld with all the comforts the local paper shop could provide; while a third resided in the

54

ancestral tablets in the home or local temple. All three spirits had to be tended lest they become the restless "hungry ghosts" that wandered the world inflicting hardship on the living.

The fortune-teller would set an auspicious date for the funeral, and a *feng shui* ("wind and water" man) would advise a burial site that would not disturb the essential harmony of mountains, winds, water and resident dragon spirits.

A man's fortune was calculated in relation to the hour, day, month and year of his birth. Each year in the cycle of 60 was denoted by a combination of one of the all-important five elements and twelve animals of the zodiac.

When a marriage was to be arranged, no formal steps were taken until the local fortune-teller had pronounced the couple's horoscopes to be harmonious. If they were not, the fortune-teller might advise his client to seek a more compatible candidate.

"This is a fire girl," he might advise an anxious mother. "She will consume a wood husband such as your son. Go and look for a water girl who will nourish him..."

unquestioned obedience

In the China of old, when a girl married, her long black hair would be swept up in a knot stiffened with resin and held by gold pins. Her rouged face was a mask beneath the tasseled, pearl-encrusted phoenix coronet. Weeks of seclusion and lamenting – for the loss of family and a familiar town or village – ended on the morning of her wedding day.

She bathed in an infusion of pummelo leaves that would wash away all traces of ill-fortune. Attended by a "good luck woman" chosen for her long and happy marriage and her capacity to produce children, she donned her wedding gown.

Later, when she left her home, she was carried across the threshold – and a pan of glowing charcoal – to ensure she took away none of her family's good fortune.

It must have seemed to the bride, that day, that everything around her was washed in the auspicious red that promised joy and good fortune. Her embroidered wedding *kwa* and silk shoes were red, and she was carried to her new home in a red bridal sedan embellished with gilt and flowers.

As the picture-book procession moved through fields of gold (for harvest was considered a good time for rural weddings) it was headed by wedding lanterns bearing the names of the betrothed. Music, gongs, drums and the chatter of firecrackers marked the route that had been planned to avoid contact with bad omens ranging from wells to widows. Meanwhile lurking spirits were distracted with scattered rice or a succulent baked pig borne before the bridal sedan.

Bearers surrounding the bridal chair carried a dowry that was the subject of much gossip and scrutiny – fine redwood furniture inlaid with marble perhaps, or camphorwood chests of porcelain and jade. The groom's family would also have broadcast the generosity of their gifts to the bride's family. Once the birth dates had been matched for harmony, gifts were presented as an acknowledgement of the betrothal.

On arrival at the groom's house the couple would pay their respects to the ancestors whose blessings had already been sought. Prior to the betrothal the birth dates of the couple had been placed beneath the ancestral tablets. The groom's family had then watched for bad omens – the death

In Old China the bride served tea to her mother-in-law signifying subservience to both mother and son.

The traditional Chinese bride – her long hair swept up beneath a tasselled, pearl-encrusted phoenix coronet – wears an embroidered red wedding *kwa* which has been elaborately worked with auspicious symbols.

of stock, or family feuds – that might indicate ancestral anxiety over the proposed union.

The young girl decked in red would have had few illusions about the life that lay before her. Owing unquestioned obedience to both her husband and mothers-in-law, she could be divorced for reasons ranging from infertility to verbosity.

Having submitted to the father who arranged her marriage to his advantage, she would now submit to the man who lifted her red veil and saw her face – sometimes for the first time.

Auspicious red – promising joy and good fortune – colours everything, from elaborate wedding candles to embroidered satin slippers, at the traditional Chinese weddings that some still choose to celebrate.

The Chinese bride would value jade above gold as a wedding gift. A pair of carved butterflies for double happiness. A jade ornament for the hair. Or a pendant carved to the contours of a fish – for the fish, being fecund and happy in its element was a symbol of happy marriage.

ty

L egend has it that even in the earth gold and jade were antagonistic, for while the appeal of gold was material, that of jade was spiritual.

Certainly no other stone in history could claim such a significant spiritual role in the life of a nation – for the limpid stone believed to link heaven and earth belonged to the realm of legend.

The Chinese believed it existed long before rivers ran or valleys reverberated with thunder. Its origins go back to the dawn of creation when the god *Pan Ku* carved the universe, becoming part of his creation at death. His head became mountains, his breath the wind and clouds, his flesh and blood the soil and rivers, and the marrow of his bones became jade.

Over the years the stone's mystique became as potent as its beauty. An emperor is said to have offered 15 cities for a jade carving he could hold in the palm of his hand. And when China was invaded by the Tartars, who subjugated the people of Han, the Imperial Dragon wept tears that petrified to jade within the earth.

Because it had the power to bridge heaven and earth, life and immortality, the emperor used a

circular Pi disc (carved in jade and representing heaven) to transmit prayers to the gods. Ancestral tablets which linked the living with the dead, were also carved in jade and when men of substance died, jade was placed in their tombs to preserve their bodies.

Chinese people value jade above any other stone, and its craftsmen are skilled at highlighting its subtle tones and striations.

The tombs of old emperors thus became a magnet for grave robbers. Those who violated the tombs of the noble or wealthy faced certain death if caught, but were handsomely rewarded for their precious plunder. Tombs were often cleverly concealed and at least one contained crossbows set to shoot automatically. This tomb contained not only the body of the emperor, but those of his concubines – and the artisans unlucky enough to know the secrets of the tomb.

Admired for its beauty and enduring strength, jade was a talisman prized by all. Even the poorest peasant woman cherished her lucky "chicken heart" finger jade that ensured fertility, and her children wore jade bangles, pendants and charms to ward off disease or the jealous spirits.

Though its smooth surface has a quality of softness, jade's fibrous texture makes it one of the earth's toughest stones, posing a challenge to craftsmen who work with delicate chisels.

Chinese craftsmen had worked with jade since ancient times and had perfected the art of revealing its subtle tones and striations. Though its cool, smooth surface had a quality of softness, jade's fibrous texture made it one of the earth's toughest stones. As such it posed a challenge to craftsmen creating a carving that expressed the inherent qualities of the stone and the hues of its spectrum. Jade ranged from pink to purple, from gold to green and even the latter boasted over a hundred different shades from "spring water green" to "moss entangled in the snow."

Marco Polo had admired the beauty of the stone carved with such skill by craftsmen in the court of Kublai Khan. However, as with the secret of silk, China guarded its jade and forbade its export. Jade was mined in only a few precious pockets scattered across the world and there is no evidence to suggest it was ever mined on a significant scale in China itself. The nephrite for carvings came from Turkestan, while Burma was the source of the emerald jewel jade, or jadeite, that women found so enhancing against the skin.

The Chinese believed that the polish and brilliance of the stone they revered represented

purity; its dense toughness suggested resolution and intelligence; its clean angles brought to mind justice; while its transparency symbolised sincerity.

And in the hands of the most gifted craftsmen, the stone of immortality seemed to possess a life of its own – an inner glow that added to its mystique.

Collectors from across the world search for rare antique jade, but out on the streets the stone of immortality carries a smaller price tag. The jade peddler, his stooped shoulders hung with hundreds of trinkets, charms, necklaces and bangles, is a walking jade shop who never lacks customers.

reverence for the written *characters*

When the first emperor of a unified China ordered his craftman to carve an imperial seal, he naturally selected jade as the material. The Seal of Succession became an enduring symbol of the right to rule – the Mandate of Heaven – and it was decreeed that only the emperor could use a seal of jade.

S eals were the most ancient form of identification, and reverence for the written characters coupled with the skill of engravers ensured that they also became miniature works of art.

The illiterate peasant would use a wooden seal to identify himself in correspondence prepared for him by the local letter-writer. A scholar might devote hours to selecting the material for his personal seal which could be embellished with a miniature bas-relief landscape or mounted by an auspicious symbol. Mandarins and military officials would issue edicts stamped with their seals – for every official had a seal of office that was closely guarded.

Seal engravers combined the skills of calligraphist with those of master carver, but the design created had to be carved within a square, circle or oblong that might measure less than two centimetres.

Painters and calligraphists were often skilled engravers, for no painting was complete without its inscription and seal. Sometimes a well-respected connoisseur would add his own personal seal of approval beside that of an artist who had created a fine painting or scroll of calligraphy.

The preparation and quality of the vermilion

used by the engraver was considered vital in the appreciation of seals. Made from pulverised cinnabar and oil, soaked on a stamp pad made from the fibres of the moxa plant, the ingredients were occasionally fanciful. The Emperor Ch'ien-lung's vermilion was made from pearl, coral, ruby and cinnabar – and his seals have not faded over 300 years.

Some of the oldest seals in China were made from bronze, but the invention of paper in the second century popularised engraving and introduced a range of materials including gold, silver, horn, crystal, ivory, clay, porcelain, amber and stone from China's most famous quarries.

Engravers combine the skills of calligraphist with those of master carver, creating miniature words of art measuring less than two centimetres across.

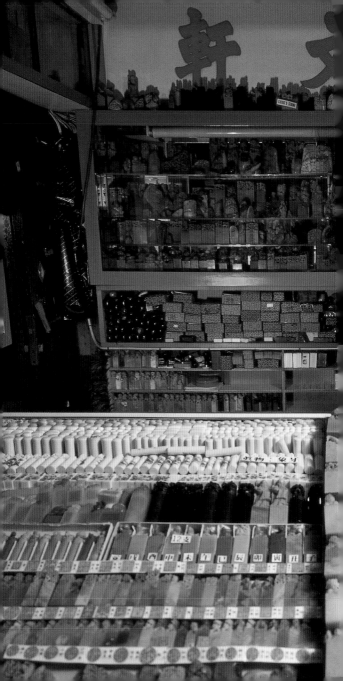

Seals – the most ancient form of identification in China – are still carved by skilled craftsmen who share a reverence for the written characters.

characters of captivating beauty

Along with paper and printing, China also introduced to the world the first civil service staffed by scholar officials. Anyone could sit the examinations for official appointments but to succeed, a scholar had to write elegant prose and poetry (which echoed the classics), be well-versed in literature, and produce fine calligraphy.

Every scholar tried to excel in painting, seal-engraving and calligraphy – but while the three were viewed as inseparable, calligraphy was considered the highest art form.

The Chinese never looked upon their writing merely as the medium of communication. The ancient pictograph formed the basis for an abiding affinity between painting and writing and turned a utilitarian sign into a character of captivating beauty.

As the slow process of shaping the script took hold, it brought with it the recognition that calligraphy could be an art in its own right. The *literati* were soon experimenting with their own stylistic embellishments to the script, but when the first Ch'in dynasty emperor assumed power in a

unified China, he swept aside such sophistication, ordering that the written language be simplified and standardised.

boldness, energy or lyricism

The invention of paper and bristle brushes (replacing shaved wood or bamboo and reed pen or bronze stylus) released calligraphy from early restraints. Now it truly flowered into an art that invited practitioners to invest each stroke, line, dash or hook with the boldness, energy or lyricism they wished to express.

Over the centuries Chinese characters have been shaped by a long process of stylization and abstraction. A character could stand alone, representing a simple object, or could be a compound of several characters expressing an abstract idea.

When a calligraphist set to work on a scroll he would envisage the brushstrokes that would break the white expanse: the powerful down-strokes, the sensuous curves, the bold dashes and the delicate lines – fine as silk – that would link one movement with the next.

The early pictograph not only communicated an image or idea, it reflected the life of the nation itself. The character for field became four plots surrounded by irrigation trenches, while that of a well – eight plots centred around a communal

well — told of the sense of communal co-operation that was the strength of a nation bound to the land.

the ubiquitous
staple

Over the centuries China's landscape was contoured, patterned and coloured by a single staple which, more than any other, nourished the hungry nation. And the rice that shaped the landscape also shaped the character of the people. For the Chinese had always lived with the spectre of famine, so they put every acre of arable land to use and coaxed the earth to yield harvests that fed more people than anywhere else in the world. Together they maintained the mud dykes that sculptured the landscape. And together they planted the seedlings, flooded the fields, transplanted and harvested the rice that later dried in the sun on rooftops.

The stored rice promised security for the circle of faces – bowls raised and chopsticks clicking – that gathered to share the morning and evening rice. And when the harvest lay gold against the backdrop of blue mountains, the people thanked the gods who had guarded their fields with vigilance and averted the droughts or floods that left their rice bowls empty.

The cultivation of rice thus became interwoven with the social, moral and religious life of the nation.

There was a time when the emperor himself planted the first rice of the season and at harvest time each village sent an annual tribute of rice to the Son of Heaven.

Over the centuries China's landscape was contoured and patterned by a single staple that both nourished the nation and shaped the character of its people.

Once a year, on the night of the winter solstice, the emperor made sacrifices to Heaven wearing an antique gold robe embroidered with sacred symbols: the dragon, sun, moon – and rice. In the early 1830s when the nation was plagued with floods, famine, insurrections – and the unwanted intrusions of

opium-smuggling foreigners from across the seas –
the Son of Heaven made a heartfelt plea to ease
China's torment. In particular the emperor requested
rain for the drought-stricken earth.

His plea, accompanied by a sacrifice of buffalo,
offerings of incense, jade
and silk, and oblations of wine,
did not go unheeded. That
very night a great armada of
purple clouds massed on
the horizon and advanced,
bringing sustained heaven-
sent rain that fell for over
a week.

Hundreds of different
varieties of rice, each with
subtly different flavours
and textures delight the
palates of the Chinese.
Though pre-packaged rice is
sold in supermarkets, many
still prefer to purchase the
ubiquitous staple at rice
shops that display each
variety in large bins –
and may also sell noodles
made from rice dough.

In the noodle factory, men are covered with the fine white flour they work with when producing the noodles that are so popular in Chinese cuisine. The rice dough can be expertly pulled and folded by hand producing a skein of fine noodles that will be sold fresh or dried, in markets and noodle shops.

Being frugal and resourceful, the people used not only the grains of rice but its flowers (as a dentifrice), its stalks (for stomach complaints), its ash (for treating wounds) and its straw (for matting, rope, paper and thatch).

And when it came to cooking the *fan* they were equally inventive. Rice was boiled, baked, steamed, fried, ground, filled, wrapped and dried. It was turned into dough which, when expertly pulled and folded, produced a skein of fine rice noodles that were sold fresh and dried in the markets and noodle shops.

Coated with a mixture of lime, salt and ash, "100-year-old eggs" – that have probably been preserved for a hundred days – are shelled and sliced when ready to eat. Their distinctive patterned shells are familiar in stalls which may also sell quail, pigeon and salted eggs preserved in brine.

記 蔎
蛋鮮

South China's earliest settlers were fisherfolk who chased shoals across the South China Seas. These hardy people dried the best of their catch for times when shoals were less abundant – and the sight of fish drying on rooftops remains common in outlying villages that still depend on the ocean's harvest.

Rice was ubiquitous in China. It dried on straw mats on rooftops or the side of the road, was carried on barges that plied the rivers, steamed in bowls at foodstalls, was served as glutinous dumplings at the Feast of the fifth Moon, and was turned into the fiery wine that accompanied banquets.

light and goodness

When the rice in the paddies deepened to emerald and then the gold of harvest, farmers never failed to hang lanterns in their fields to frighten off malevolent spirits. For in China the lantern was a symbol of light – of Yang – and no social or religious celebration was complete without displays of auspicious red lanterns.

ometimes villagers combined the two powerful symbols of light and goodness into the form of a 100-foot-long "dragon lantern." As many as 80 jointed lanterns, suspended from poles, separated snapping jaws and thrashing tail. As the dragon lantern snaked through the fields it was accompanied by a fearsome cacophony of drums, gongs and exploding firecrackers.

From ancient times a Lantern Festival welcomed the light and warmth of spring, and later, when summer's heat was eclipsed by the cool of autumn an essentially feminine festival ushered in the prettiest of lanterns. During the Moon Festival young girls burnt incense and candles and whispered prayers to the matchmaker on the moon, but for the children the delight of the festival was the lanterns. At Moon Festival time the lantern maker truly indulged his flights of fancy with symbolic lanterns (butterflies for longevity, lobsters for mirth) in the shapes of birds, insects, fish and animals.

In old Peking there was a famous street of lantern stalls which, on market days, was festive with colour. Rich and poor came to Lantern Market Street, for lanterns had always been considered indispensable in China. The humblest peasant would not venture out at night without one, and mandarins and military officials, traveling across the country in sedan chairs, always displayed their titles on the lanterns that lit their paths.

Lantern-makers, whose families had practised the craft for generations, were constantly devising new designs and trying new materials for their handiwork. Fancy silken lanterns, tasseled and ornamented with pearls or jade, were fashioned for wealthy mandarins. Silk or paper lanterns, exquisitely

The eclipse of summer's heat by the cool of autumn has always ushered in the most magical festival of the lunar year. On the night of the Moon Festival, young girls burn incense and whisper prayers to the matchmaker on the moon in the glow of fanciful lanterns.

The lantern is a symbol of light – of Yang – and no social or religious celebration is complete without colourful lanterns in symbolic shapes. Lantern-makers, whose families have practised the craft for generations, constantly indulge in new flights of fancy to light the festivals of the lunar year.

Since ancient times, festive lanterns have welcomed the warmth of spring, and the cool of autumn. During the Moon festival in autumn the lantern-maker fashions symbolic lanterns: butterflies for longevity, lobsters for mirth.

painted with scenes from legends, appealed to connoisseurs. However the simple man contented himself with a basic lantern of bamboo and waxed paper, or a lattice-work lantern fashioned from split bamboo covered with waxed paper coated with glue and varnished to transparency. Lanterns were also made from wood, gauze, glass, transparent horn or even stalks of wheat. There was even one – which military men might favour – on which figures of warriors on horseback (set on a revolving base) endlessly chased one another as the candle's hot air rotated them. But the simplest lanterns were those made by children in autumn when ancestral graves were swept and made ready for winter. Candles were set in the hollow of lotus leaves. They glowed green and gave untold delight – if only for a night.

There was a time when most of the windows of China were made of paper pasted damp over the wooden lattice frames – in much the same way as lanterns. The paper was replaced at Chinese New Year, when small red "window flower" papercuts were pasted on the inside of the new windows.

When dusk fell and lamps were lit, each simple house became a large-scale lantern, each street a place of instant beauty and gaiety.

Or so it must have seemed to lovers and poets...

a priceless heritage

Chinese lanterns – so simple, so magic – have cast their glow down thousands of years of Chinese history. And they still light festivals today, in China and in Chinatowns throughout the world. But no one knows if the lantern-maker will continue creating his fanciful designs into the future; no one knows how these "echoes of old China" will fare in the 21st century.

Certainly, traditional Chinese shops still add colour and character to cities around the world, but their chances of survival seem tenuous. Though Chinese temples still lure people of all ages, paper shops are dying with the generation of worshippers who demand them. While traditional medicine shops are busy and have revealed ancient cures for contemporary complaints (sea horses are also efficacious for high cholesterol levels!) the bone-setter concedes he has no young apprentice to whom he can pass the skills he acquired from a master, or the knowledge accrued through years of practice. While tea houses still add a distinctive noisy clamour to city streets, the tea shop, its containers filled with aromatic blends, may well be swallowed by supermarkets or upmarket gourmet shops.

Chinese people have always had an insatiable appetite for the new and innovative. Cities such as Beijing, Singapore and Hong Kong have made it their business to be in the forefront of both the production and consumption of 21st century technology. In the race to embrace modernity, the old is being razed and replaced with little thought of its historical and cultural significance. And so, even in China itself – where temples and tombs, courtyard homes and heritage gardens are being bulldozed to make way for high-rise apartments, shopping malls and highways – no one is gambling on the future of trappings and traditions that are links with an almost fabled past.

What is certain is that if these "echoes of old China" entirely disappear, the cities that surround them will have lost much more than just a little "local colour."